NOW I'M READY
A WOMAN'S GUIDE TO KNOWING WHEN A MAN IS READY TO COMMIT

BY BRYANT WRIGHT

(c) 2017 by Get Real & Get Free Publishers

ISBN-13: 978-1979168137
ISBN-10: 197916813X

Printed in the United States of America.

N♡W
I'M READY!
A Woman's Guide To Knowing
When A Man Is Ready To Commit
BRYANT
WRIGHT

FOREWORD

In this simple, but skillfully designed handbook, Bryant has been charged with the task of explaining the stages and phases of relationship building. From the flirt all the way to the altar, he has given us a pluralistic view of how women react based on the actions of men. This is a must read for people from every walk of life and for people currently involved in any phase of a relationship. This book provides the litmus test to confirm if couples are on the right track or if they need to make adjustments along the way. When a man is ready to commit, the woman MUST be prepared to respond.

Gloria Barksdale, CEO & Founder

Get Real & Get Free Publishers

DEDICATION

I dedicate this book to everyone who has inspired and supported me on my journey: My daughter, My family, My friends and my coaching clients. You stood by me during this process of writing and finishing this book. You gave me ideas that would be a benefit to those who encounter this book, that would give them knowledge, hope and be a guide for them.

To my daughter Heaven. You are an amazing, beautiful princess that I am so proud of. You have grown so much and are maturing more and more each day. I wanted to dedicate this book to you because I know one day that when you are finished with school and you start your journey to courting someone, that this book will be of great benefit to you when it comes to knowing when a man is ready for commitment and marriage. You still have a lot growing to do, college to finish and some more experiences to go through in life but I wanted to make sure that you have this guide that when that time comes, you will be prepared. I love you Princess.

DEDICATION (2)

To my friends. When I was going through the storms, you were there to cheer me on, and let me know that the storm that I was experiencing wasn't going to last. You told me to stay focused on the bigger picture, of getting the book done, because there were so many that would need to read this book that would bring about a change in their life.

To my family. I love you all, for the encouragement and inspiration that you have poured into my life. I have received a lot of support from you and I am glad to have you as a part of this journey. Thank you for giving me advice and direction, that has shaped me into the man I am today and has prepared me to help those that I come across in life.

To my clients. I thank you for allowing me to take you by the hand and take you to the next level, and after helping you get through many breakthroughs, you continually asked when was I going to write a book that could help others, and I persisted to say that it's coming, and now I can finally say that it's here.

ACKNOWLEDGEMENTS

This book would not have been possible if it was not for you Jonathan Sprinkles. I knew I had a message but I didn't know exactly how I was going to deliver it or how to go about putting it together. I remember meeting you the first time at your Presentation Power boot camp and you taught me how to connect with people and show them why you care. You showed me the importance of finding solutions to problems that would help people become better.

Thank you, LaTesha Rogers, for pushing me to keep writing the book. When I was going through storms, you were there to keep me focused on what really matters. You let me know that people needed to hear this message that people were going to benefit from my book; I just had to show up. There were times I thought I would never get the book done, but you pushed me to get it done and for that I thank you.

ACKNOWLEDGEMENTS (2)

My dear friend Carmelo Scotty Ramos. You are the one that believed in me when some didn't and you kept saying that you and I were going to make it one day and share our message with the world. You were there during my trying times, and in the midst of all I was going through, you kept encouraging me to believe in myself. Thank You!

Stacey Flowers, when I met you, I knew there was something that was captivating about you and I didn't know what it was at first but the more that I got to know you, I finally realized that it was your drive, determination, and direction that I was drawn to. When I was thinking small, you came along and said Bryant, "You need to think bigger than what you are thinking". You asked me if I wanted to change the world, and I said "Yes! I do!" and you said, "Stop playing small and get out there and think big". I can now say because of you, I thought bigger and this book is just a part of what things have happened and things that are to come. Thank You!

TABLE OF CONTENTS

Chapter 1: Affection

Words

There's something unique when a man can speak life into you. What words is he saying to you to build you up and also build others up? It's important to recognize what he says when he speaks to you and others. This is important because you want someone that has the ability to speak good things over you and not put you down.

Does he use words that are helpful and beneficial for your growth in the relationship or does he use words that tear you down and will end up making this an unhealthy situation?

When you make mistakes, how does he talk to you? Does he belittle you or build you up, because whatever words he speaks to you, is what he believes about you!

Questions

The words that he says to you;
do they make you
feel uplifted or belittled?

If he happens to say something
that isn't uplifting,
is he humble enough to apologize
for his actions?

Does he use encouraging words
to support you in what you do?

BOTTOM LINE

A man that knows the importance
of positive words,
will speak life into you and not
drain the life out of you.
He knows that whatever he
puts out, that he will get
back and saying the right words
to his women will
make her feel loved, respected
and welcoming.

Physical Touch

Touch is a natural part of life from the moment we are born into the world. Hugs, kisses, hand-holding, gently slapping each other when laughing and talking are all signs of "good" physical touch in a relationship. When both share in all of these types of physical touch, the stages of the relationship begin to shift in a direction of permanence.

Escalation in physical touch leads to intimacy which is the highest form of physical touch in a relationship which should be saved for the stage of marriage. More often than not, many couples become involved sexually before they can really discover who each other is emotionally or socially and sometimes the relationship suffers early because of this.

It is more important to understand each others joys and woes, likes and dislikes, idiosyncrasies and uncanny ways first before engaging in a hurried sexual relationship.

Women get suspicious and sometimes uncomfortable with a man who is anxious to become sexually intimate before showing signs of emotional, physical and spiritual protection and covering. Physical touch has its limits before knowing if the man in the relationship is serious about the heart of the woman.

Questions

When you and him are walking
together, does he hold your
hand, or hold you close to him?

Does he show physical affection
without you
even asking him too?

Does his touches feel inviting
or uncomfortable?

BOTTOM LINE

A man that is into you loves to
show physical touch
towards his woman. He's not
shy about letting her know that
he is into her physically and he
does it without being
asked to do so.   However, the
woman must not be pressured
into a sexual relationship until
she knows he has her heart and
will protect her when the
relationship escalates.

Gifts

Inside of a man dwells a natural born instinct that makes him want to buy and do special things for the woman that he loves, or genuinely cares about. Even after the chase is over and he "has her" he will still feel compelled to  do these things. Why? For men, loving and giving go hand in hand. When you are the object of a man's affection he is always looking for different ways to shower you with presents whether they are big or small.

Does the man in your life find pleasure in surprising you with gifts, even beyond holidays and special occasions? Is he constantly on a mission to do things for you that will ultimately put a smile on your face? As you ask yourself these questions, remember that the  value of the gift is not what's important. The point is that, if he is attempting to go out of his way to make you happy, then whatever he gives is priceless.

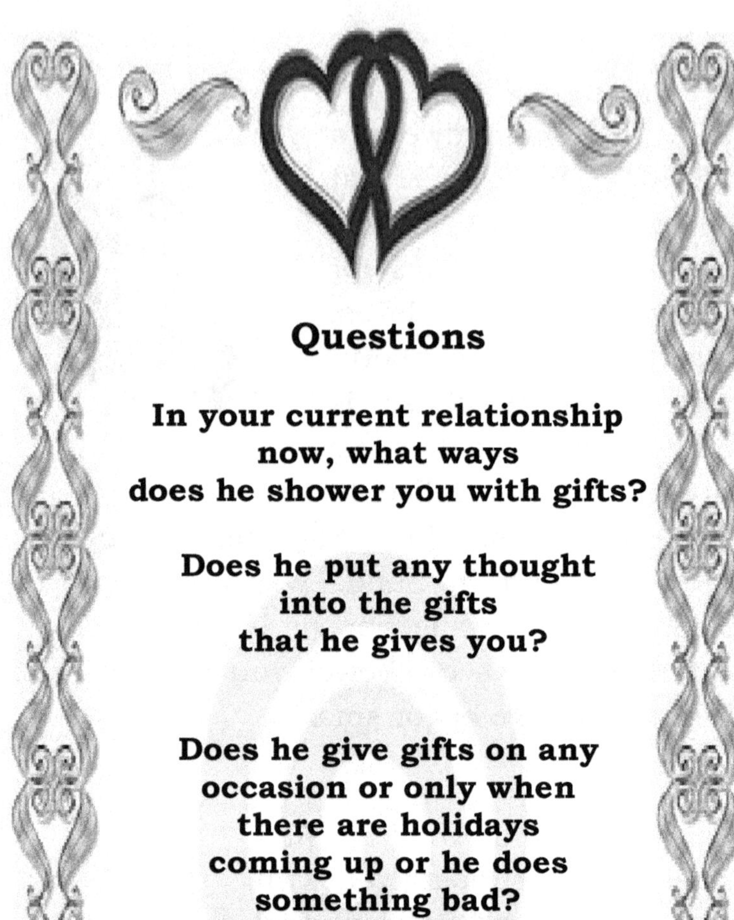

Questions

In your current relationship
now, what ways
does he shower you with gifts?

Does he put any thought
into the gifts
that he gives you?

Does he give gifts on any
occasion or only when
there are holidays
coming up or he does
something bad?

B O T T O M   L I N E

A man that appreciates you,
will in some way give you gifts.
If he is not doing it, have the
conversation on why he doesn't
buy you things.
There could be an underlying
reason but
most importantly don't settle
for an excuse.

Chapter 2: Emotionally Ready

Creates Own Happiness

Many times in life we rely on others to create our happiness and if a man does not know how to create his own happiness then he will try to search for happiness in a person and if he is not fulfilled he will continue to look for happiness in someone else instead of creating his own happiness that he desires to have.

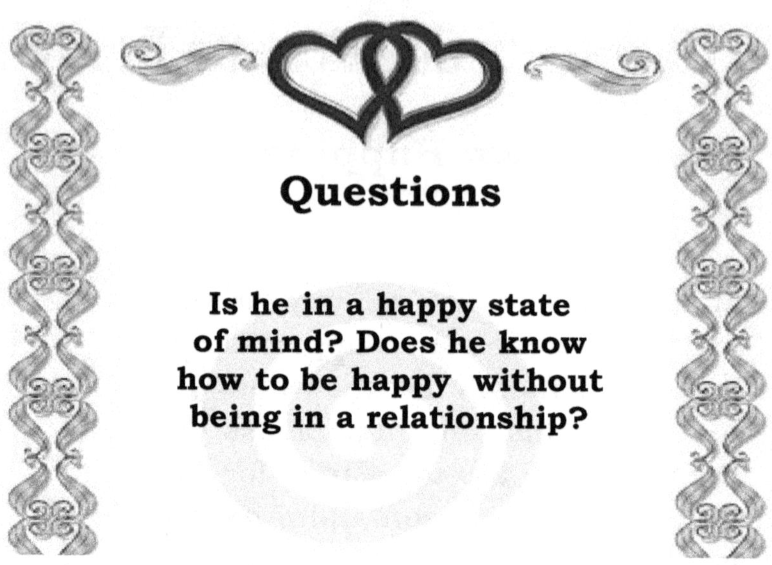

Questions

Is he in a happy state
of mind? Does he know
how to be happy without
being in a relationship?

BOTTOM LINE

A man must be able to create his
own happiness
because when it comes to a point
in time that you are not able to
make him happy, and has not
mastered in making himself
happy, he will always feel
the need that you are there
to create that happiness for him.
It is true that we do in a way
make others happy by
the actions we do but
in the end, it is his
responsibility to create his own.

Loyal

In this world, we know that it has been hard to find someone who will remain loyal to you. Knowing that, you want to make sure that the person that you are planning to spend the rest of your life with has the capabilities of remaining loyal. In the dating phases, most times you can see a person is loyal when things are going good, but what about, when things go bad? Can this person stand the test of time, when put into

an uncomfortable situation, or will they not let it get to them and they will have the staying power of remaining loyal to you.

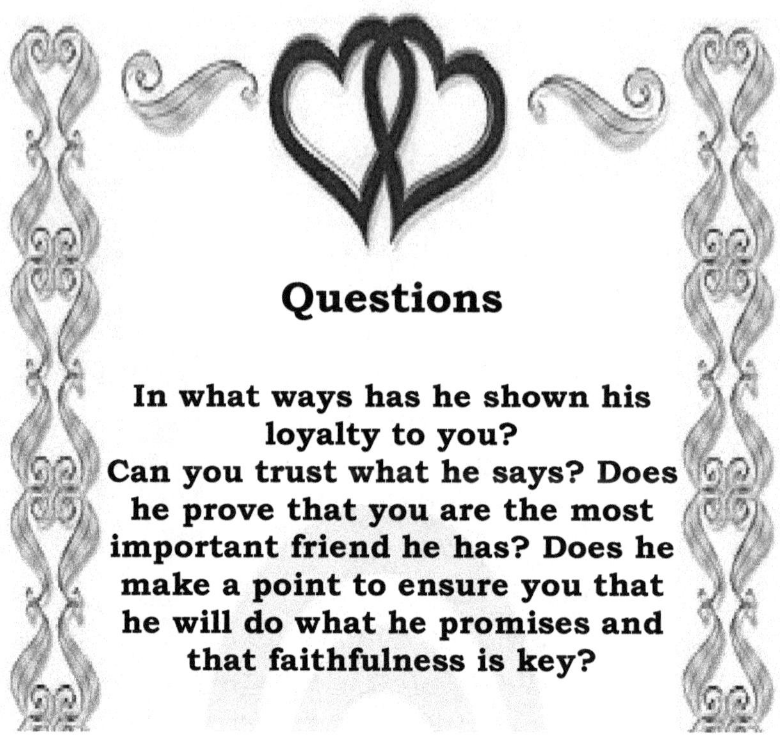

Questions

In what ways has he shown his loyalty to you?
Can you trust what he says? Does he prove that you are the most important friend he has? Does he make a point to ensure you that he will do what he promises and that faithfulness is key?

BOTTOM LINE

A man that is loyal purposes his words and his time to prove to you that you are the apple of his eye. His faithfulness in word and deed become obvious. He makes sure to check in with you, honor his promises and commits to proving you come first. Loyalty and faithfulness are two main ingredients that cement a happy relationship with longevity.

Knows Himself

A man that has gone through life will eventually know himself. Every man is different in knowing when this happens but when it happens, there are some important signs you should look for to let you know that he knows himself. A man that doesn't know himself is more likely not to know exactly what he wants in life, when it comes to career, relationships his spiritual  walk and other things in life we deem important. He will always be back and forth with himself if he doesn't know  exactly what he wants and he'll test and try different things in life just to find himself. This can be dangerous because if you are involved with a person like this, they may give you the run around in the relationship. You need someone that knows exactly who he is and what he wants because when he knows that, he is more likely to have a foundation.

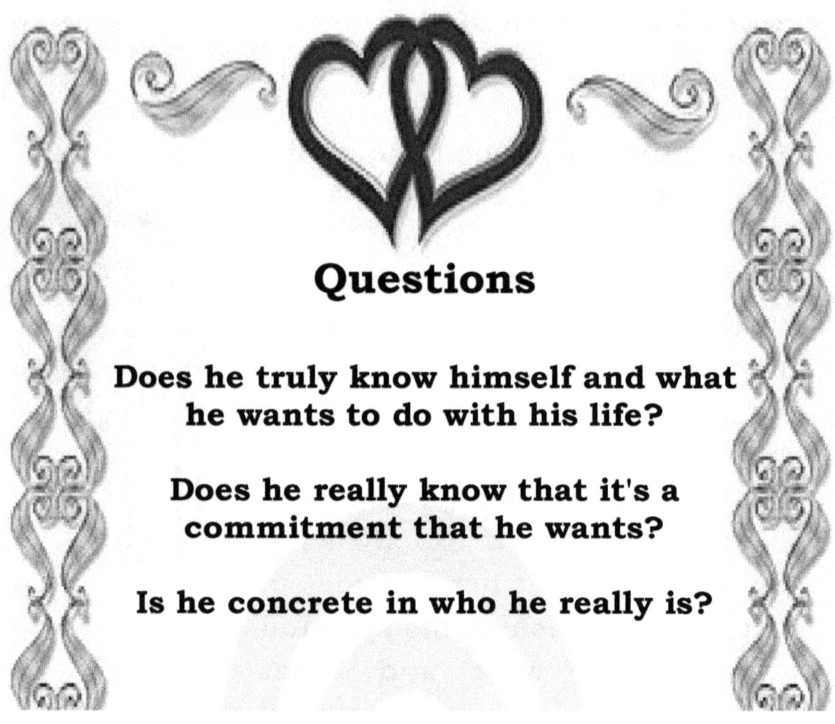

Questions

Does he truly know himself and what
he wants to do with his life?

Does he really know that it's a
commitment that he wants?

Is he concrete in who he really is?

B O T T O M   L I N E

A man that knows himself
will show signs of it.
He won't have you wondering
if this is really him,
or is he putting on some type
of front.

Faces Problems

As you are dating the guy that you feel could be the one, take notice of how he handles problems. Why is this important? This will let you know that when he is faced with problems, will he stay and face those problems or will he run away. In life, you want to be sure that who you are committing to

is down for you for the long haul, that is willing and ready to fight through those problems and not easily give up on situations. This will let you know that this person is willing to do any and everything to find solutions instead of making excuses and leaving the situation.

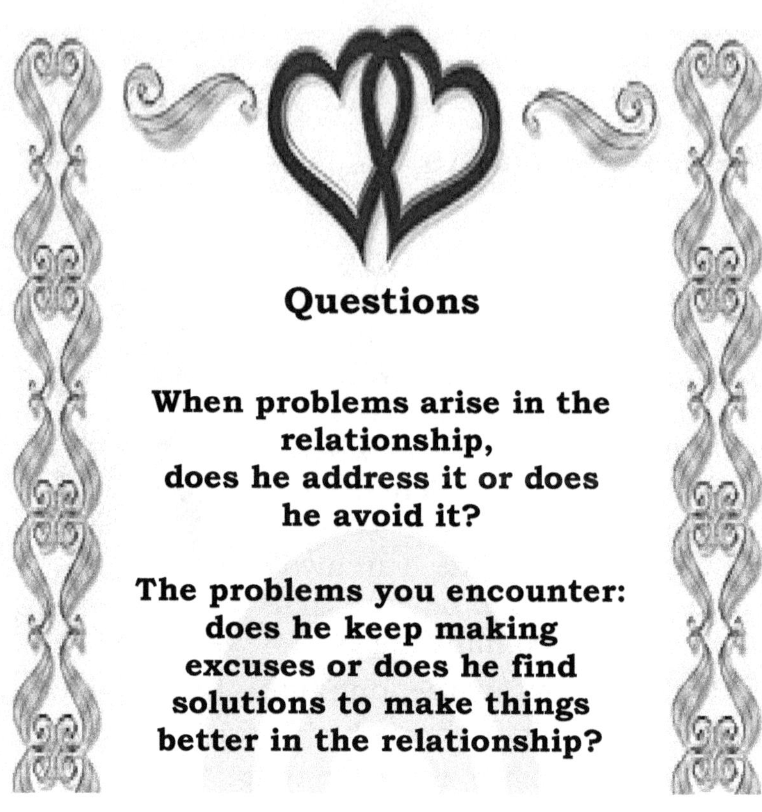

Questions

When problems arise in the
relationship,
does he address it or does
he avoid it?

The problems you encounter:
does he keep making
excuses or does he find
solutions to make things
better in the relationship?

B O T T O M   L I N E

A man that knows how to
face problems is someone
to consider for a relationship,
because it shows that even
though you may be going
through some situations,
he is willing to fight them
with you to weather the storm.

Healed

When a man has experienced brokenness in past relationships, and before he starts a new one, the question has to be asked. Is he healed? Sometimes men, start a new relationship, believing, that the next person will cover up the hurt that the last person caused. He hasn't taken the time to heal from his last relationship. This can be dangerous if he has not properly healed. He will continually reflect on past relationships and if it comes to a point that you do something similar to what an ex did, he will start to compare you to them and start to feel as if he is going through the same thing again. Some ways to tell if a man is healed from his past relationships is to listen to how he talks about his past relationships. Does he sound bitter or is he harboring any hurt that he has not forgiven them.

Questions

When you have conversations about
your ex's does he respond in
a bitter way?
Has he truly forgiven those
that have wronged him in
the past?
When you have disagreements,
does he bring up
his ex's comparing them to
you saying you're just like my ex?

BOTTOM LINE

A man that is truly healed will let
it be known on how he treats you
and in his conversations
of the past. If he keeps bringing
up old situations that make
him upset or he treats you like
others in his past relationships,
then he has not truly healed yet.

Soul Ties

Has he cut it off? In his past relationships, has he been able to sever all of what came with that relationship. Anytime we have a relationship with someone we give a piece of ourselves to the other person , physically, spiritually, emotionally. When he broke 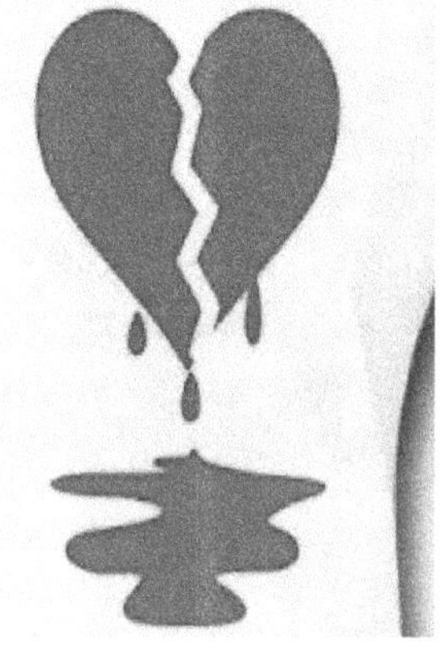 the other relationships off was he able to sever the ties with those he had a relationship with. Why is this important. If he has not severed the ties with the other people, he will bring all of what he took from another person and bring it into a new relationship.

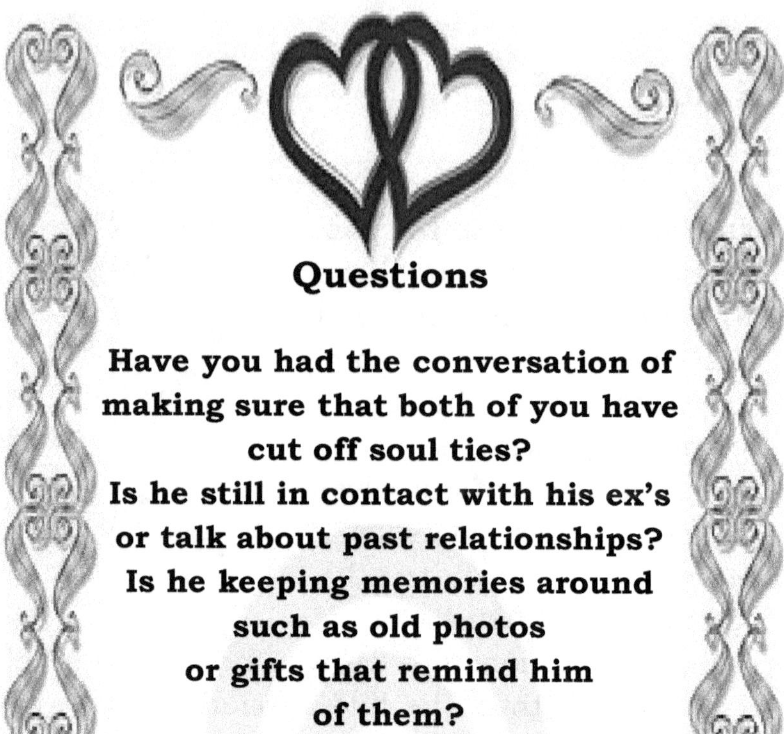

Questions

Have you had the conversation of
making sure that both of you have
cut off soul ties?
Is he still in contact with his ex's
or talk about past relationships?
Is he keeping memories around
such as old photos
or gifts that remind him
of them?

BOTTOM LINE

The subject of soul ties is so
important because when you have
not properly cut those people
out of your life, you can bring
those ties into a new relationship
and it can make the
relationship dysfunctional because
the person is not truly giving
their all to you and leaving
pieces of himself to his past
relationships.

Chapter 3: Future

Friends Know

Once you shift your focus, time, phone calls, text response time, and other "traditional" tracking habits by your friends, your friends KNOW that something has changed your life! It is important for respect and friendship maintenance purposes, that your friends know that someone who you have strong, different or more permanent feelings for has entered your life. They need to learn early on how to respect your decisions, your time and your need for exclusivity with this NEW person that you plan to get to know better. Make a decision early on to respect those who respect you and your personal/private time with your new love, and be ready to release those out of your life who choose not to respect your decision. In either case, sometimes the inclusion of or loss of friends may come with tears, mixed emotion, fear and joy!

Questions

Has he brought up the topic of
meeting his friends?
Does he sound excited about
introducing you to his friends?
Does he introduce you as his
girlfriend to his friends when
you first meet them?

BOTTOM LINE

A man that is into you will soon
want to tell all his friends about you,
and want to bring you around them
so he can show them exactly
who he is with and who he is very
serious about.
If he isn't trying to introduce you to
his friends then it's
very possible that he doesn't see a
future with you. A man that sees
a future is quick to show you off,
but if not, he will keep hiding you.

Uses "We"

When a man is thinking of his future with you he begins to 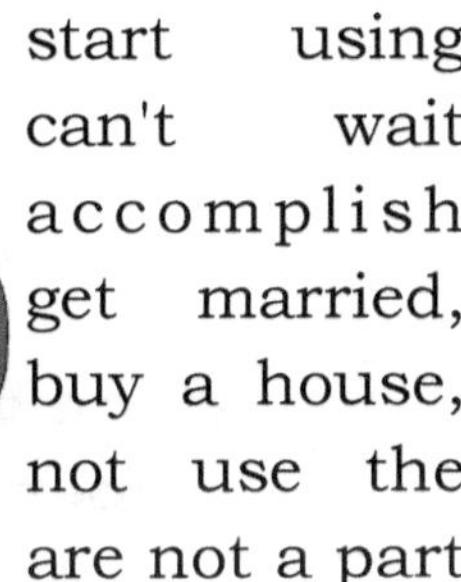 start using the word we. I can't wait until we accomplish these goals, or get married, start a family, buy a house, etc. A man will not use the word "we" if you are not a part of his future. When he starts to use the word "we", he has made up in his mind that he wants it to be you and him together and he sees a life with you. Using the word "we" is a word of involvement and if you don't hear those words from the man you are with after a certain amount of time in the relationship then he doesn't have plans for to make it about the both of you but only about him.

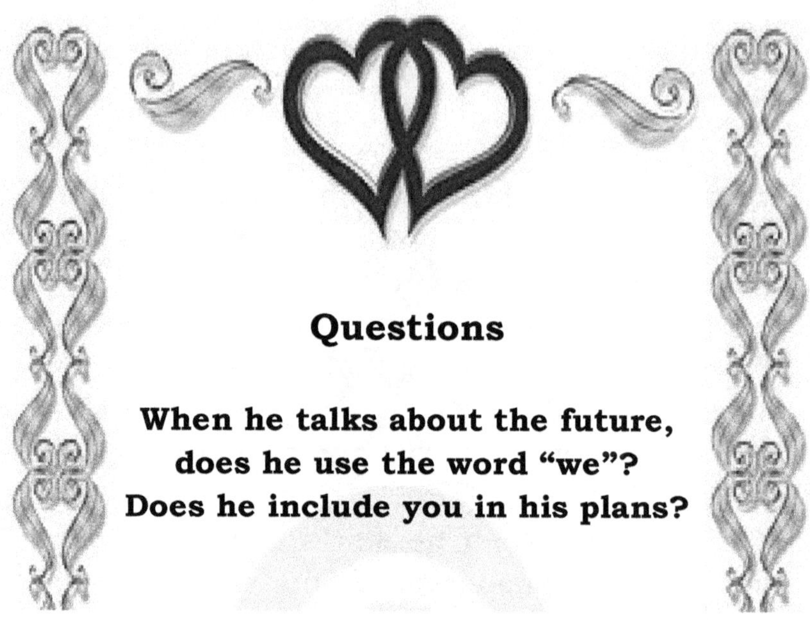

Questions

**When he talks about the future,
does he use the word "we"?
Does he include you in his plans?**

BOTTOM LINE

A man that is looking at a future

**with you will start
to use the word we at some time
during the relationship.
If he continues to use the word
I in his conversations when you
talk about present
and future plans then somewhere
there is a disconnect.**

Exclusive

When a man is serious about you ,he will let it be known that he wants you and him to be exclusive. He doesn't want anyone else to have the chance of coming a long and swooping you up, so he will let it be known that you are the one. No games no guessing, he will let you know. If they are not ready, they will take you on this roller coaster ride throughout the

relationship making it seem like it may lead somewhere but in all actuality, it's not going to go anywhere. Men are not shy about what it is that they want and who they want, so if you find yourself asking constantly where this relationship is going, the answer is **"Nowhere!"**

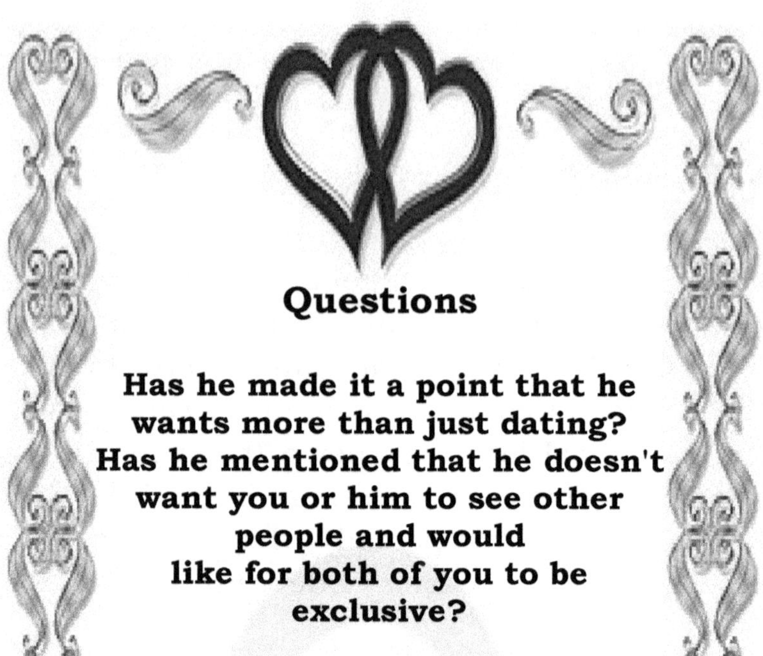

Questions

Has he made it a point that he
wants more than just dating?
Has he mentioned that he doesn't
want you or him to see other
people and would
like for both of you to be
exclusive?

B O T T O M L I N E

A man that could only see
himself being with you and
nobody else will make it clear
that he
wants to be exclusive.
He will know exactly
what he wants and won't
beat around the bush or leave
you wondering if
this is leading anywhere or not.
His objective will be to pursue
you any means necessary to
make it known that he wants
a future with you.

Outings

Although many people enjoy "dating" at home with the lunches, dinners, movies and other quiet time activities, nothing speaks more loudly to the presentation of love for a woman than outings. Being seen in public holding hands, smiling, eating out and other such venues gives her the security that you are happy to be seen with her and that you want everyone to know that she may be that "special someone."

Regular outings whether spontaneous or planned also speak to his wanting you to know you are a valid and valuable part of his life. Being seen often in public means that he is proud to have chosen you to walk by his side, be a part of his daily existence and to confirm to others that exclusivity exists. You are his walking, breathing affirmation that love truly exists and that he is selflessly ready to commit.

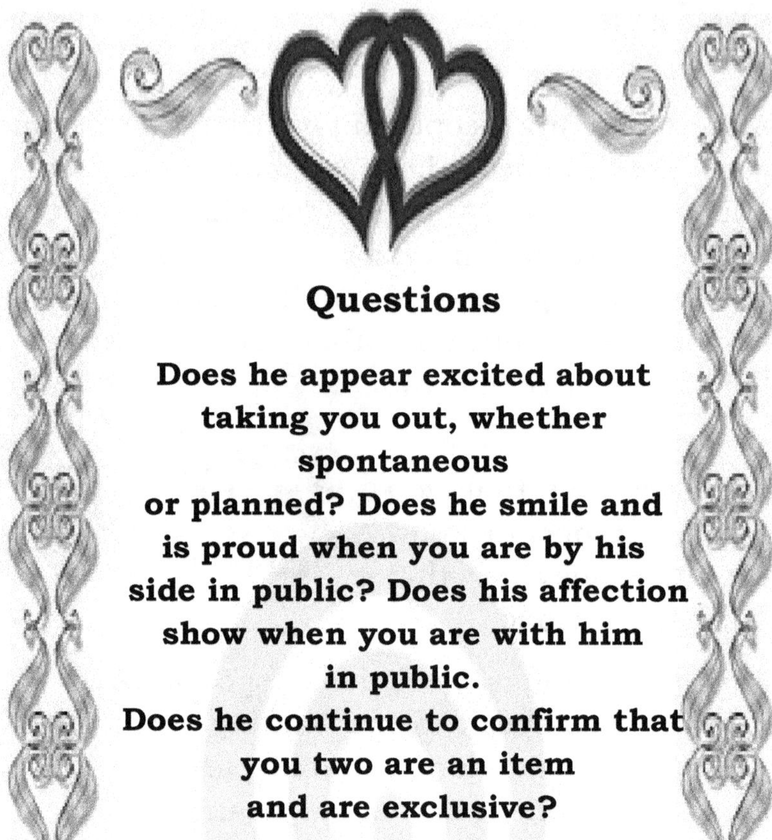

Questions

Does he appear excited about
taking you out, whether
spontaneous
or planned? Does he smile and
is proud when you are by his
side in public? Does his affection
show when you are with him
in public.
Does he continue to confirm that
you two are an item
and are exclusive?

BOTTOM LINE

A man who creates purposeful
outings and includes you in his
plans is ready to let the world
know about his find. After
showing you off to friends, family
and even co-workers, he is
working on leading you down the
aisle to present you publicly and
display his love for you to the
masses.

Meet Family

One of the greatest signs that a man is serious about lifelong commitment is when he is excited about introducing you to his family. Whether family embraces you immediately or not, this statement of presentation and introduction  is the segue, in most cases, to implying that you will be the one and only that he will want his family to know he has chosen for his life. Family approval or the lack thereof should NOT always the ultimate decision maker for a man who has already placed his choice in his heart.

Questions

Is he excited about introducing
you to his family?
If not, why is there a stigma
against his wanting to
introduce you? Is it important for
you to find out what happened in
the past to cause family to
doubt his choices?

B O T T O M   L I N E

A sure sign that he is willing and
ready to make you his wife is his
excitement about introducing you
to his family. Observe their behavior
and reactions towards you, but
do NOT allow their reactions to
deter your feelings for him
if you know he is the one.

You're His Best Friend

There should be no walls or secrets between you before you walk down the aisle. Many relationships wear out or fail when there is lack of trust. Be able to trust him as he does you with everything. When you can work out differences and handle misunderstandings AND deal with idiosyncrasies BEFORE marriage, then friendship  abounds in your marriage. Whoever was the best friend on either side will now have to take a SECOND seat alongside the love of your life. They should NEVER be used to come between or be involved in making decisions relative to your relationship. A three-tied cord includes you, her and God.

Questions

Does he begin to call you his best
friend after weeks or months of
your bonding while sharing your
joys and woes? Does he tell
others that you are
his "new" best friend
and that he enjoys getting
to know you?

B O T T O M   L I N E

A man who calls you his best
Friend and even denies time
with his original best friends
is ready to call you his wife.
When he has difficulty trusting and
confiding in you BEFORE marriage,
he will continue this discomfort
after marriage and lean to outside
sources for advice and consolation.

Marriage Talk

Sometimes a guy won't necessarily bring up marriage in the form of speaking about it but instead has it in his mind that this is the one he wants to marry and will plan to pop the question one day. There are some things you should look for in the relationship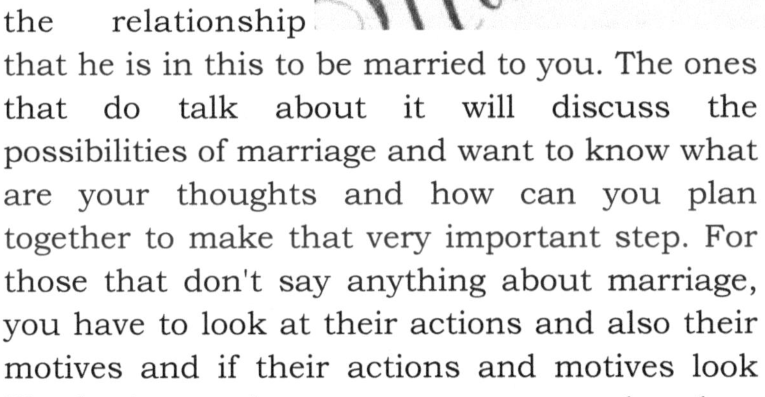 that he is in this to be married to you. The ones that do talk about it will discuss the possibilities of marriage and want to know what are your thoughts and how can you plan together to make that very important step. For those that don't say anything about marriage, you have to look at their actions and also their motives and if their actions and motives look like he is wanting to marry you one day then this is a good sign.

A man that is not ready will never bring it up and he may use the words that he just wants to be friends and see how everything goes. If you bring it up and it's uncomfortable to him, there could be several things that could have triggered that. Either you brought it up too early in the relationship or his motives are definitely not leading to marriage.

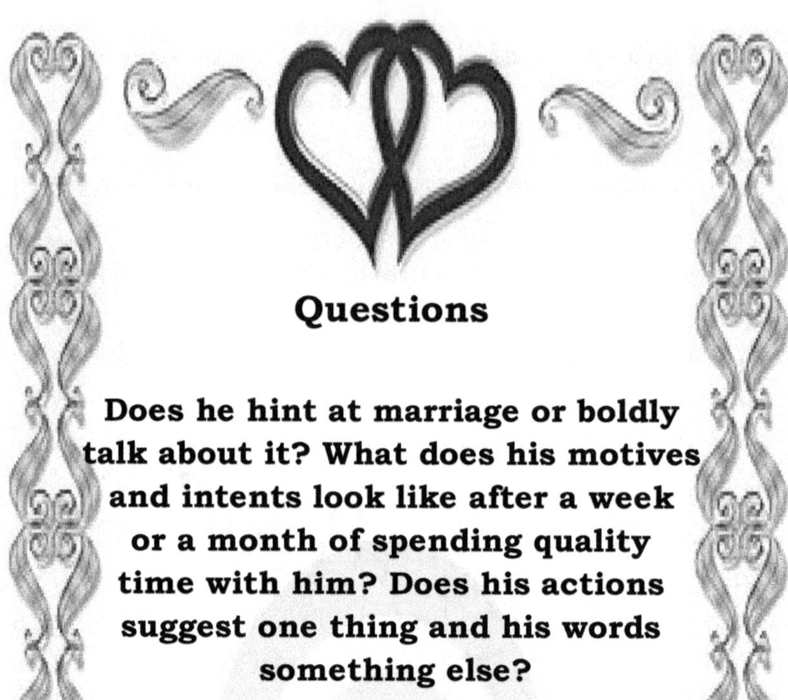

Questions

Does he hint at marriage or boldly talk about it? What does his motives and intents look like after a week or a month of spending quality time with him? Does his actions suggest one thing and his words something else?

B O T T O M   L I N E

A man who slowly or boldly talk about marriage has the right motive for making you his life upfront. Suggestions about your life's goals, desires, ring size, clothing choices, relocation, children, favorites, finances and other "lifestyle" goals are sure signs you are heading in the right direction of marriage.

Chapter 4: Priorities

Availability

A man interested in pursuing you for marriage will sacrifice time and make purposeful decisions to ensure his availability for you. He will find time throughout his day to text, flirt, call, email, use messenger, Skype, Facetime or do whatever it takes to let you know you are in the forefront of his mind.  Long distance relationships, in particular, sometimes suffer the most when one or the other is constantly distracted, has a busy work schedule, children or elderly parents they care for, or find themselves involved into many activities or organizations. The adage "absence makes the heart grow fonder" can quickly change to "out of sight, out of mind" and many relationships start drifting when there is not enough contact and communication by any means. Being up close and personal is best when establishing a relationship but when there is separation for whatever occasion, communication by any means is important when two people are working on life goals together expecting to spend eternity together.

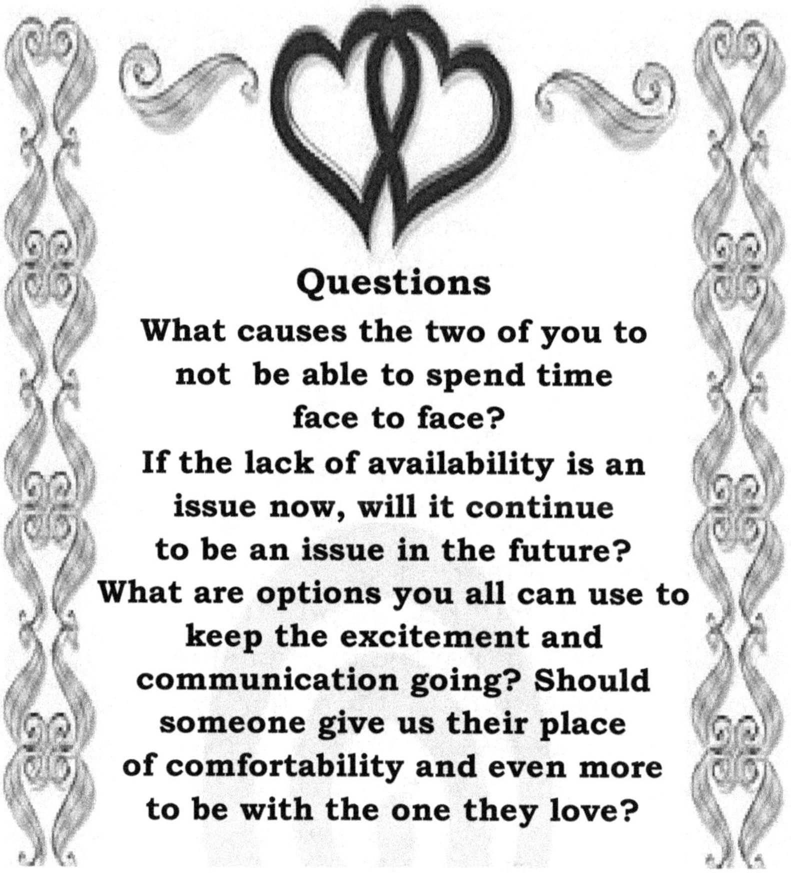

Questions

What causes the two of you to
not be able to spend time
face to face?
If the lack of availability is an
issue now, will it continue
to be an issue in the future?
What are options you all can use to
keep the excitement and
communication going? Should
someone give us their place
of comfortability and even more
to be with the one they love?

B O T T O M   L I N E

Depending upon the situation and
circumstances and who has more
to lose financially, relative to
stability and what they bring to the
table, may be the litmus test to
who should make the greater
sacrifice for the sake of marriage.

Easy to Reach

This can go along with availability but in some ways it is different. They can be available, but not able to reach easily. When you call him, does he pick up the phone. If you can not reach him at the time,  does he make it a point to get back to you as soon as he is available or at least text you to let you know that he seen your text and when he gets a chance he will respond accordingly. Never put yourself in a position where you have to play phone tag with the person that you are with.

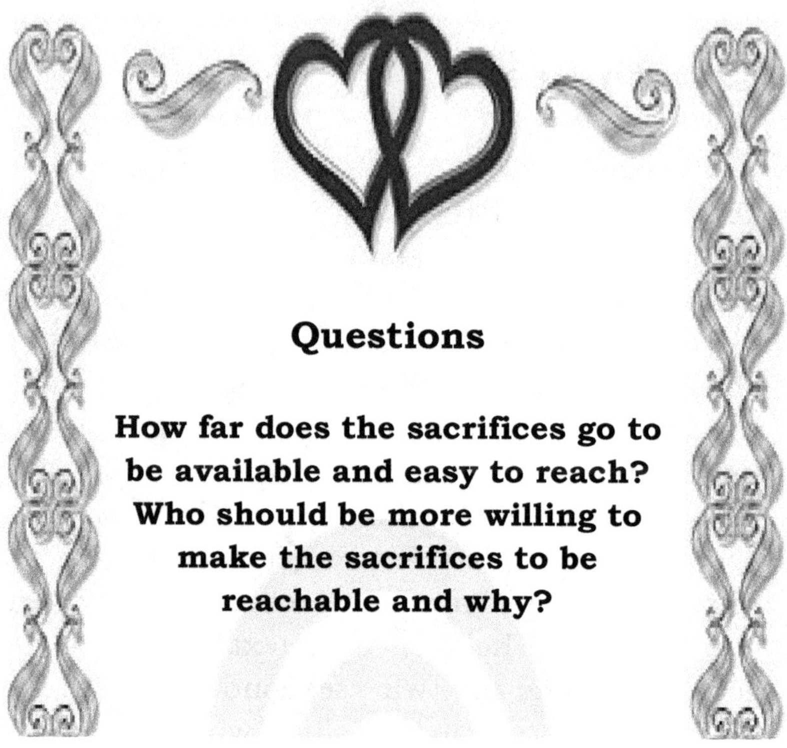

Questions

How far does the sacrifices go to
be available and easy to reach?
Who should be more willing to
make the sacrifices to be
reachable and why?

BOTTOM LINE

Even if life dictates major
Distractions along the way,
there needs to be
established sure fire ways to get
back to each other in reasonable
periods of time.

Follow Through

When he says he is going to do something, what happens when it's time  to deliver. A man can say all the right things to you but can he deliver on his promise. We have heard time and time again, that actions speak louder than words and it is in his actions that will let you know if he is the type of person that follows through. You don't want someone that constantly promises you things and never comes through. When you have that type of person in your life, you will constantly battle him, in wanting him to follow through. A person either has integrity or not and you want a person who will know that when they say they are going to do something, that they're going to deliver on their promise.

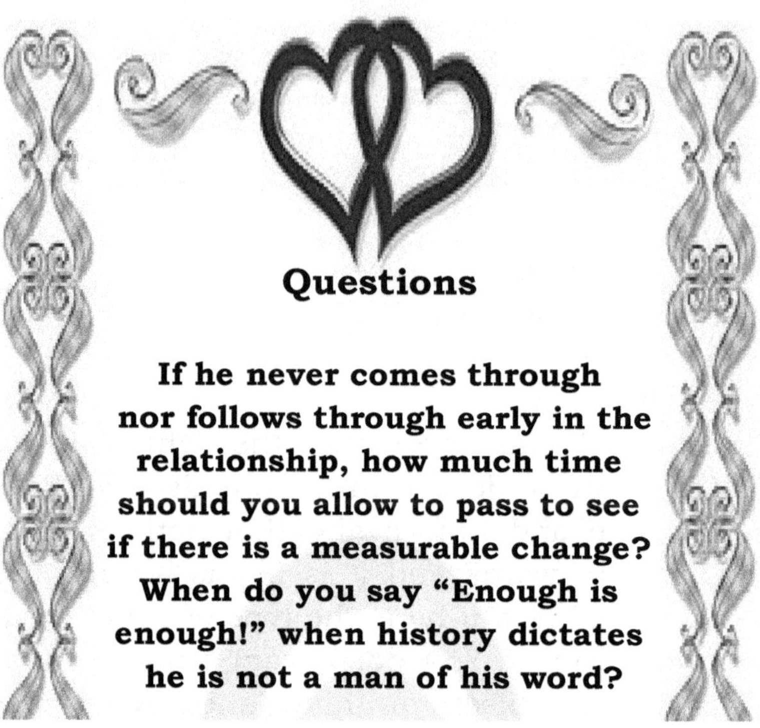

Questions

If he never comes through
nor follows through early in the
relationship, how much time
should you allow to pass to see
if there is a measurable change?
When do you say "Enough is
enough!" when history dictates
he is not a man of his word?

B O T T O M   L I N E

Follow through must be a main
aspect of trust and protection in
a relationship especially for a
woman. When she sees a
man follow through, then she
can trust him to be a leader,
protector and provider.

Chapter 5: Spiritually Ready

Relationship With God

The most powerful scripture and revelation relative to marriage is found in the 22 most important words ever spoken on marriage. These words are found in Genesis 2:24: "Therefore shall a man leave his father and his mother, and shall cleave unto his wife: and they shall be one flesh." The next important line that is even more powerful is "she shall be called woman because she was taken out of man." Genesis 2:23.

The three main principles of a Godly marriage indicate that a man must LEAVE his parents, and CLEAVE to his wife. This means above all else that NOW he is PHYSICALLY, EMOTIONALLY, and ECONOMICALLY ready to take care of his wife and future family because he is SPIRITUALLY ready. He has a relationship with God, can hear his instructions and follows them to the best of his ability. In order to be protector, leader and provider successfully, he must be able to walk with God like Adam in the cool of the garden and make both short term and long term plans to be accountable in his marriage.

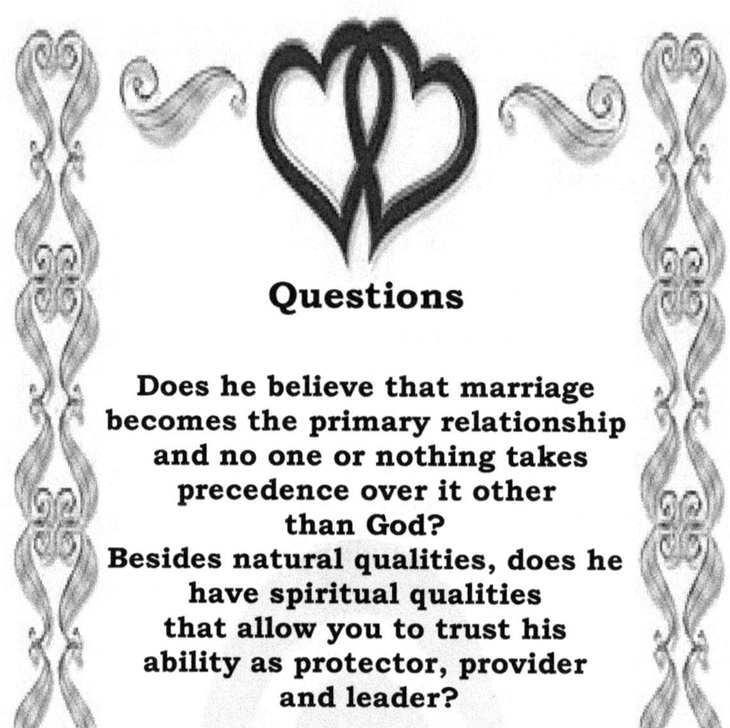

Questions

Does he believe that marriage
becomes the primary relationship
and no one or nothing takes
precedence over it other
than God?
Besides natural qualities, does he
have spiritual qualities
that allow you to trust his
ability as protector, provider
and leader?

BOTTOM LINE

A three-tied cord must present
itself in the establishment of man,
woman and God. A man without
relationship with God cannot
successfully take care of a woman
that God has prepared to be
his wife. Adam was asleep when
God did spiritual surgery on him
and pulled out of his womb his
help meet. Many lose sight of God
as Lord over their lives and the
family suffers as a result
of this neglect.

Leader

The bible declares that a woman should submit to her own husband. It also states that she is the "weaker" of the two vessels which means that even in his weakness, he is still designed to lead. A woman submits more easily to the man who shows the true skills of a leader, than to one who does not. A man who leads in love is an extreme turn on to a woman. It becomes easy for her to submit, honor, respect, trust and YES, obey him, when he is loving in his leading.

A man who becomes a dictator and/or diminishes the role, emotions and esteem of the woman he says he loves, soon becomes abusive, neglectful and disrespectful. Hence, a dishonored vessel can no longer be trusted as a leader and the heart of the woman becomes bitter, and she in turn scorned. Once trust and loss of love sets in, the relationship is destined to crumble and fall. Besides the issues surrounding finances and the handling of money, abuse, neglect, and bitterness is the second leading cause of divorce.

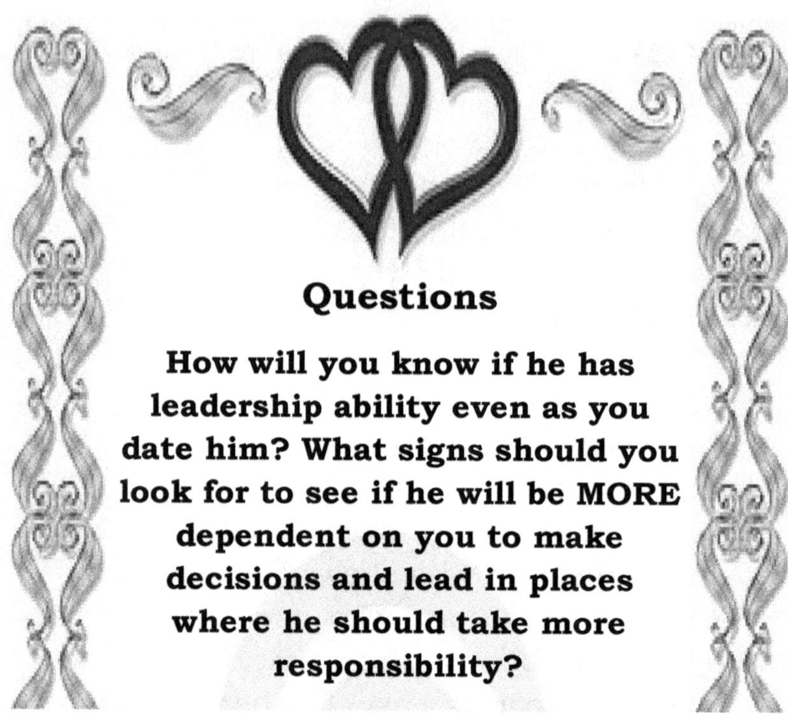

Questions

How will you know if he has leadership ability even as you date him? What signs should you look for to see if he will be MORE dependent on you to make decisions and lead in places where he should take more responsibility?

B O T T O M   L I N E

If he does not show leadership skills and ability early in the relationship and he relies on you to make most of the decisions, then more likely he is going to be a dependent instead of a leader. A woman wants a man who will take charge, make a decision and stand by his decision relative to household business. He must show her he can operate in wisdom and in love while providing stability even if he has to lean on her as his help meet from time to time.

Provider

A man who knows how to provide for his family has become the standard dream family man exemplified down through the years as the "perfect man." When a man has a strong work ethic and makes sure the household is taken care of in every aspect, the woman usually has no

An "UNPRODUCTIVE" man has no business being in a "PRODUCTIVE" woman's life.

problem with being the "help meet" when she is called to be. Even as a contributor of the household provision, the woman looks to the husband as the one who makes the necessary adjustments to provide for himself, his wife and the children who become a part of it. The less stress put on a marriage through provision, the more fluid and loving it's maintenance.

Questions

How will you know if he is or will
Be a provider even as you
date him? What signs should you
look for to see if he will be MORE
dependent on you to make
provision when he should take
more
responsibility?

B O T T O M   L I N E

If he does not show skills
and ability early in the relationship
to be a provider, and he relies
on you to make most
of the decisions, then more likely
he is going to be a dependent.
A woman wants a man who will
take charge, make a decision
and stand by his
decision relative to providing for a
household. He must show her he
can operate in wisdom and in
love while providing even if he has
to lean on her as his help meet
from time to time.

Chapter 6: Financially Ready

Whose Money is it Anyway?

Debt has proven to be the leading cause of divorce. Learning to be disciplined in the area of money has proven to be the major challenge of couples when there is no conversation, counseling, nor creative measures taken to secure finances moving forward. Counseling is very important when the topic of money comes up so that it is clear how money from both parties will be used, spent, saved and managed.

Goals should be set up front and explicit agreements should be made as to who will pay what bills, from which accounts, and then how finances will be shared or spent for shopping, food, travel, entertainment and the like. Decisions on how much is placed in a joint account and how each person will save or keep for themselves individually should also be shared. Disagreements and secrets in the area of money always lead to distrust, disdain, disturbance and ultimately, divorce, in MOST cases.

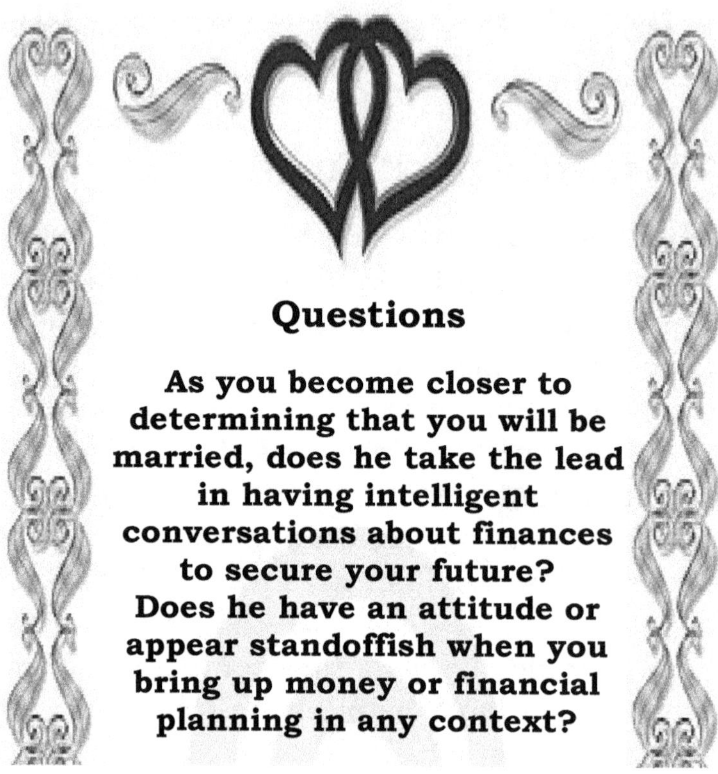

Questions

As you become closer to determining that you will be married, does he take the lead in having intelligent conversations about finances to secure your future?
Does he have an attitude or appear standoffish when you bring up money or financial planning in any context?

BOTTOM LINE

Watch for signs in his reaction when you are ready to speak about finances and financial planning for future goals

early in the relationship.
If he is a spend thrift, extremely frugal or seems to be an impulsive spender, he may need counseling in that area if he does not receive what you have to say about his spending habits.

Relationship Readiness Chart

Phases		Stages
The Flirt	→	The Considering
The Date	→	The Calling
The Kiss	→	The Caressing
The Love	→	The Captivating
The Knowing	→	The Connecting
The Covering	→	The Claiming
The Engagement	→	The Committing
The Counseling	→	The Confirming
The Marriage	→	The Convening

Note: The Engagement and The Counseling can change hands and/or share both stages of Commitment and Confirming.

Appendix A: Phases & Stages

Phase/Stage 1:
The Flirt: The Considering

The flirt is usually the first sign that he is considering you. No matter what level of consideration at the time, the flirt is the first sign that there is some type of interest, attraction or need to be in your face and in your space. The moment glares, smiles, second looks, or words are exchanged, the flirt has ignited the opportunity towards sharing names or even phone numbers. This opens up the dialogue for more information. This phase usually happens quickly and you will know by his gestures if he will continue to allow or refrain from additional contact.

Phase/Stage 2:
The Date: The Calling

The follow up in the form of a phone call, text, messenger, in-box or any other personal method of contact helps determine whether or not the new meeting will be considered a friendship, relationship, a mere acquaintance or nothing at all. By dissecting what is said, how it's said and its reactions or comments to statements made, the man or the woman will either be excited, slowly emerging or totally disinterested usually by the end of the first full conversation or the first date. Depending upon the trust level of either party, that will determine how much information is shared and shift the relationship into another gear or digress it back to the level of acquaintanceship.

Phase/Stage 3:
The Kiss: The Caressing

Usually after the second or third meeting, get together or date, men have a tendency to want to at least hand or cheek kiss her for the first time. The first hug and kiss seem presumptuous and most women are still cautious until they are able to validate much of the shared information in previous conversations first. They need the security in knowing that whatever he shared early on is truth so that trust can continue to be developed. Depending upon how quickly the emotional attachment develops will dictate when the kiss of passion begins. More often than not, the man is more ready for the kissing and caressing regime than she is.

Phase/Stage 4:
The Love: The Captivating

He is captivated by you when you find him calling, visiting, texting, or dating you often. The attraction and attention he's giving you now may be overwhelming but you will also feel the desire to call, visit, text and see him more often. When you speak to each other on the phone, you can feel him/her smiling back. When you are in each other's presence, you finish each other's sentences, reach at the same time, laugh at the same things, and in most cases, like the same foods and activities.

Like the honeymoon phase of the marriage, the captivating is the cement, the love that holds the relationship together. It is the magnet that secures and affirms that you have shifted into more than just friendship and that you are closer to marriage. At this point, the two of you are seeing the same things and heading in the same direction. This "captivating" must be nurtured, not only during the dating phase, but even throughout the marriage. Without it, many marriages fall short and fail too early. As the expression goes, whatever you did to get her, the same or more you should do to keep her.

Phase/Stage 5: The Knowing: The Connecting

Your knowing speaks directly to lifelong commitment when your captivation has shifted to spending time with each other day and night. You want to go everywhere, do everything and let everyone know that you two are an item. You do everything from dancing, movies, walks in the park, attending family functions, and even going to church together. The unity becomes more evident and the connecting becomes easier to handle because you recognize unity in force.

Phase/Stage 6:
The Engagement:
The Committing

So now! After all of the adjustments, changing your life around, spending exclusive time with her, including family and friends, having sleepless nights, heart skipping beats, and sacrificing your way of thinking in so many ways, the most vulnerable moment has arrived. Before you lose your nerve (lol), you are ready to "pop the question!" A number of mixed emotions produce waves of anxiety, fear, additional sleep deprivation along with the joy of knowing that you have found that "special someone," that "soul mate," your "better half," and all the other colloquialisms that come with knowing this is the person you want to marry.

The engagement comes with a standard to now be set to fast forward your life. Plans for her usually begin with an immediate need to share the news, plan for living arrangements, shift the dynamics of her life and decide on the wedding's who, what, when, where, and definitely how. Now that she knows that all of your promises are ethical and you have proven yourself to be dependable, reliable and that perfect person for her, the submission process begins and the spirit of covenant is in full force now.

Phase/Stage 7:
The Counseling:
The Confirming

"To be or not to be?" is definitely the question that resounds in the hearts of couples ready to go all in. Questions begin to flow and the ultimate decision to be all in and go all the way is the premarital counseling. It is relatively the icing on the cake or the ultimate confirmation that you are dotting your i's and crossing your t's to ensure that you can have the best "perfect" marriage that two "imperfect" people can have.

In most counseling sessions, 12 major topics or any derivation/combination are discussed and avenues for adjustment in any of those areas are suggested or recommended so that the couple can be clear on where they stand. These topics usually include:

- ❖ *Your Marriage Commitment*
- ❖ *Life Long Goals*
- ❖ *Mutual Expectations*
- ❖ *Living Arrangements*
- ❖ *Children/Blended Family*
- ❖ *Money*
- ❖ *Parents and In-laws*
- ❖ *Gender Role Expectations*
- ❖ *Sex and erotic moments together*
- ❖ *Conflict Resolution*
- ❖ *Spiritual Life*
- ❖ *Extramarital relationships/affairs*

> Make it your goal to create a marriage that feels like the safest place on earth.
> — Greg Smalley

Phase/Stage 8:
The Marriage:
The Convening

Ladies, once he has popped the question and put a ring on it, this is the surest indication that he finally knows! Once he agrees to counseling and takes the man position to move forward, then you know that the convening is shifting your life forever. Covenant is defined as an agreement, usually formal, between two or more persons to do or not do something specified.

Traditionally, we must pledge our love, produce a license, have the witnesses and confess our vows publicly to seal the deal. The woman traditionally wears white to indicate not only virginity in many cases, but to indicate that she is moving forward into her "new" proudly covered by the one who will cover her soul, protect, take care of, and love forever. The words spoken on this day, known as the "vows", whether written or repeated indicate that the convening begins and is expected to last forever. This is the official time to wear the title "Mr. & Mrs." indicating that the seal cannot be broken especially if it is sealed by God and witnessed by man.

Summary and Survey

There are many stages that relationships go through and there are many resources that provide their version of what these stages may be. Summarize and survey your relationship and prepare to engage in the necessary counseling or training you may need to be successful at any levels of these stages before moving forward. Here is a short list of some of the versatile stages you may currently find yourself in:

Stage #1: The infatuation
Stage #2: The knowing
Stage #3: The stage of disagreements/conflict
Stage #4: The adjustments
Stage #5: The merging stage
Stage #6 The happy stage
Stage #7 The stage of doubts
Stage #8 The engagement stage
Stage #9 The stage of complete trust/marriage

Take the time to really understand your highs and lows, what needs to change or what can remain the same. It is in the best interest of both in the relationship to take the time to really understand your highs and lows, what needs to change or what can remain the same. It is in the best interest of both in the relationship to REALLY KNOW what can be considered acceptable and which direction both of your lives will take once committed.

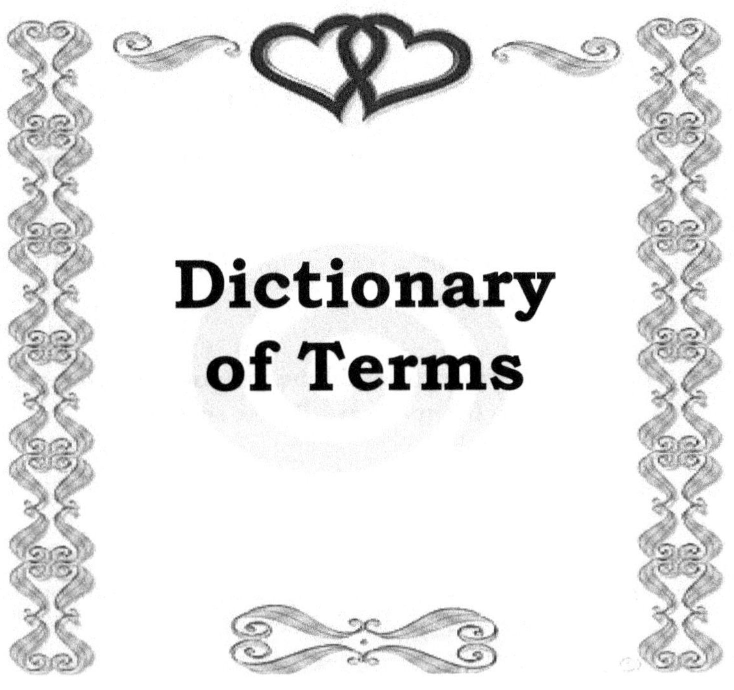

Dictionary of Terms

For purposes of this book, here are the definitions of term
used to support this writing.

Terms	Definitions
Affection	fond attachment, devotion, or love: emotion; feeling; sentiment
Calling	the act of a person or thing that calls; a summons
Captivating	to attract and hold the attention or interest of, as by beauty or excellence; enchant
Careening	to lean, sway, or tip to one side while in motion
Caressing	an act or gesture expressing affection, as an embrace or kiss, especially a light stroking or touching
Confirming	to establish the truth, accuracy, validity, or genuineness of; corroborate; verify or to acknowledge with definite assurance
Connecting	to join, link, or fasten together; unite or bind to establish communication between
Consciousness	awareness of one's own existence, sensations, thoughts, surroundings; the thoughts and feelings, collectively, of an individual or of an aggregate of people
Counseling	professional guidance in resolving personal conflicts and emotional problems

Dictionary of Terms

Terms	Definitions
Covenant	an agreement, usually formal, between two or more persons to do or not do something specified
Covering	something laid over or wrapped for concealment, protection or warmth
Coveting	to wish for, especially eagerly
Date	a social appointment arranged beforehand when a romantic relationship exists or may develop
Engagement	a betrothal or promise to marry
Flirt	to court triflingly or act amorously without serious intentions; play at love
Honeymoon phase	the month or so following a marriage or any period of blissful harmony that diminishes in times and seasons
Kiss	to touch or press with the lips slightly pursed
Love	a profoundly tender, passionate affection for another person or sexual passion or desire
Marriage	interpersonal union to form a familial bond that is recognized legally, religiously, or socially
Phase	a stage in a process of change or development
Stage	a single step or degree in a process

About the Author

Bryant Wright is a transformational speaker and relationship expert who was born and raised in Akron OH, but currently, resides in Las Vegas Nevada. He specializes in relationship coaching and has a passion for helping others learn how to reestablish healthy bonds built on the foundation of three principles; love, trust, and communication. However, it wasn't always that way.

After experiencing a few broken hearts and failed relationships, he decided to take a step back to reevaluate himself to see why love wasn't working in his favor. He began to read self-healing books while attending various workshops and conferences that could somehow help him to find the missing pieces of how relationships work. It wasn't until several years of gathering information and long hours of research that he was finally able to apply all that he had learned to begin the journey of helping himself along with helping others. Since then, Bryant has gained 7 years of experience and even personal growth in his own relationships and has held hundreds of seminars, trainings and private sessions with friends, family, and coworkers who have all benefited from his unique coaching style.

About the Author (2)

His enthusiastic coaching approach guides singles and couples into, building and establishing, long lasting unions for the purpose of leading to marriage. Through his distinct teaching, you'll learn abstract skills that will help you to deeply love yourself first, and then in turn; focus on truly loving others. Bryant has made it his life's mission to make prosperous relationships attainable to everyone.

When he's not coaching clients or speaking in front of an audience, Bryant loves to sing, play the piano, and spend time with his family and friends. He also likes to travel and experience different cultures and their cuisines.

www.ingramcontent.com/pod-product-compliance
Lightning Source LLC
Chambersburg PA
CBHW070814280726
48660CB00015B/740